Plainchant

Plainchant

poems

Eamon Grennan

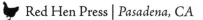 Red Hen Press | *Pasadena, CA*

Book layout by Daniela Connor

Library of Congress Cataloging-in-Publication Data

Names: Grennan, Eamon, 1941– author.
Title: Plainchant: poems / Eamon Grennan.
Description: First Edition. | Pasadena, CA: Red Hen Press, [2022]
Identifiers: LCCN 2021046230 (print) | LCCN 2021046231 (ebook) | ISBN 9781636280134 (trade paperback) | ISBN 9781636280141 (epub)
Subjects: LCGFT: Poetry.
Classification: LCC PR6057.R398 P53 2022 (print) | LCC PR6057.R398 (ebook) | DDC 821/.914—dc23
LC record available at https://lccn.loc.gov/2021046230
LC ebook record available at https://lccn.loc.gov/2021046231

The National Endowment for the Arts, the Los Angeles County Arts Commission, the Ahmanson Foundation, the Dwight Stuart Youth Fund, the Max Factor Family Foundation, the Pasadena Tournament of Roses Foundation, the Pasadena Arts & Culture Commission and the City of Pasadena Cultural Affairs Division, the City of Los Angeles Department of Cultural Affairs, the Audrey & Sydney Irmas Charitable Foundation, the Kinder Morgan Foundation, the Meta & George Rosenberg Foundation, the Albert and Elaine Borchard Foundation, the Adams Family Foundation, the Riordan Foundation, Amazon Literary Partnership, the Sam Francis Foundation, and the Mara W. Breech Foundation partially support Red Hen Press.

First Edition
Published by Red Hen Press
www.redhen.org

for Deirdre and Tommy and Anne, and to the memory of our dear brother, Dermot (1948–2019). And thanks as always to my life partner Rachel.

CONTENTS

Plainchant

Encounter

Knacky keen and swift was the flighty hare that flitted almost up to me in Fogarty's near field where I tried to stand still as a post so he might stop and stare at me with his basalt-black burning eyes, ears upright as antennae, and balance erect there before me, as if the sunny morning itself had conjured both of us out of air, out of thin air that I took in like a sudden shot of whiskey then held, breathless . . . but he simply glance-swerved, agile as any fighter jet, then away with him between the mud-spattered green ridges of the next field, to be all headlong leg-elbowed dash beneath the barbed-wire fence into the out-of-sight, leaving only his ears to me as if pointed and pencil-sketched on the clear air until they too faded as I followed my own bent and pondered the blue sky and the sea's ribbed dish of green and blue blown glass, heart still singing from that encounter, which I'm packing away now in these plain words—to be taken out at times of need: the stop, the suddenness of the coming and going, the whole morning woven like a wreath around basalt-black eyes, brown cantilevered legs: a swerve, a knacky dash, a racing into—before I could cry *Hare!*— invisibility.

Singer in Storm

Your question—your answer—
your song, what does it know?
—Celan

When in the stormy wet morning a blackbird
lands on our erratic-looking young birch and
perches there, gazing off at air that's been
gray-swaddled by a raincloud swallowing up
lake and hill, then I'm struck by the simple
endurance of the small heart that composes
its own song and lets it out through the tiny
open passage of its throat and golden bill as
if it were a song of praise, a praise-song
absolute and abiding, never mind what the
weathergods could concoct and cast at us:
such a small act but it seems of defiance and
love—if that's the word—of the life he's
been given, come into: the one moment he
finds at each breath-beat and must, it seems,
relish . . . and I wonder how, in his double
life of stress and song, he keeps himself
together and free (as any straitened single
life might) with instinct and habit directing
each of his quick food-seeking hops across
the mown grass, scaring away a single shy
dunnock before lifting off and being lost to
me again in the gray-opaque rain-thickened
swirl-about air.

Chance

Lovely, aren't they? . . . Sweet, too, already,
is what she said, the woman I met by chance
on my morning walk as she was reaching an
arm clear over brambles to pluck another
plump ebony-glinting blackberry from a
tangle of briars growing by the narrow lane
to the sea. *Here,* she said, turning back to
me, *Have one*—holding the flat of her out-
stretched hand out to me, from which I took
(trying not to touch the soft center of her
life-lined left palm while noting the three
rings on its fourth and middle fingers—one
a simple band of silver or white gold,
another glistening with tiny green diamonds,
the last a small sapphire oval) took one
blackberry, and when she said *Take another*
I took another. *Lovely, thanks,* I said,
walking on then and saying, and hearing her
say as she walked away in the opposite
direction, *See you* . . . each of us delivering
the farewell that's conventional around here,
which all know is not to be taken literally,
and I could (knowing she was turning the
corner that would put us out of sight of each
other) could lick my stained lips at the in-
tense brief sweetness of the fruit and feel the
slight hardness of the one seed that lodged
between two teeth, which my tongue (hard
as I tried) could not dislodge.

Lark-Lustre

Gravity-defying, the lark in the clear air
of a June morning stays aloft on a hoist
of song only, and only when song goes
as breath gives out does the bird let
itself down the blue chute of air in such
an aftermath silence so profound you'd
think it was a double-life creature: one
life aloft in blue, all clarity, the other
hidden in the green swaddle of any
rocky field out here where, when
summer happens, you'd almost see the
long silver ribbons of song the bird
braids as if binding lit air to earth that is
all shadows, to keep us (as we walk our
grounded passages down here) alive to
what is over our heads—song and
silence—and the lot of us leaning up:
mind-defeated again, just harking to it.

Spiderlight

These, our resident spiders, it seems,
have a refined sense of belonging—
webbing even the bristle-head of the
kitchen broom I lift to whisk from
the open skylight (through which
bright daylight is pouring) a tangle of
their thickened webs that have been
cross-woven into those camouflaged
predatory traps set at angles where
glass meets wood and where moths
and flies must be blinded to un-
wariness by the inrush of daylight, or
(in the far-from-blind spider-night)
lulled to blundering into the net that
is both deadly concealed weapon and
post-mortem larder, rewarding the
lurking patience of the spiders that
remain at home in their waiting game
where—after attending to short-lived
panics of heated buzz and
struggle—they'll wrap and store in
silk the day's or the night's fresh-
caught catch, then sleep until the
next desperate do-or-die shiver of
web-strands wakes them again to the
necessity of their savage, unsparing,
clinical business.

Renvyle Couple

When the big cob with great loud water-slapping wing-flaps leans all-forward to achieve liftoff, with his long compass-wavering neck, intent head and massive white wing-rush skimming the cobbled surface of Lough Rusheenduff, the sound of his beating wings above my head was not a bell-beat, no, but a series of sharp explosive reports as of huge hands clapping an old slow dance of their own untaught devising, before the airborne bird soared then leveled off, banked, and landed with hardly a splash, then turned with majestic ease and (slowly but decisively) started to sail across water, with the south wind behind like a servant steering him towards the small green island where his gazing mate, who had watched the whole flaunting show with who knows what mixed feelings, waited with their small brood of furry brown cygnets tucked in convoy-close: her intent eyes all knowing expectation, instinct-in-coupledom knowledge . . . all patience.

Seals off the White Strand, Renvyle

Cold dark deep and absolutely clear . . .
—Elizabeth Bishop, "At the Fishhouses"

When I saw—close to shore where
the opal-colored quiet sea like a
lazy cat was effortlessly lapping—
the heads of three seals (small slick
domes with an inset glitter of lava-
black eyeballs, the brows barely
skimming the still surface of the
incoming calmest tide in weeks) I
wondered if I should (like Bishop
on the rocky cold shore of Maine)
sing to them: not one of those
Baptist hymns she knew by heart
about the virtues of total immersion,
but a song from this side of the
same ocean—*The Lass of Aughrim*
maybe—making its tale (of love and
loss) croak plaintively in the bare
air, hoping the seals might surface
to hear how humans coped in song
with their saddest stories . . . and then
I thought too I might dip my hand in
that chill baptismal water, to feel
the burn of it, even taste as she did
its bitter brininess—thinking all the
while the seals might lift in species-
sympathy their own high, amphibian,

melancholy voices into this our un-
hindered open air and sing along
with me: though in the end I just
stood and gazed at those three pitch-
eyed salt-slick hound-heads gazing
unblinking back at me, as if waiting
patiently for something, anything—
anything in either world—to
happen.

Near High Tide

On the White Strand someone has artfully inscribed
a mare and her foal in damp sand, both in profile:
something ancient, cavelike, and tender about their
long-necked, large-headed, graceful stance and how
the young one's head is reaching up and out to
nuzzle its mother's nose: so simple and absolute
they are in this, their one caught moment by that
unknown sketcher, which the advancing tide will in
less than two minutes now erase, as I'll walk away
watching my own shadow: first dark, then pale, then
disappearing as that polished afternoon sun-disk is
swallowed up in one dark-charcoal mountain-flank
of cloud.

Entering Omey with Rachel and Kira

First we cross the pools and ridges left at low tide by
the vanished ocean, then on to the Island itself, a
silent haven in this sunny late-September quiet, the
light itself grown sandy where we advance between
hedges and low stone walls bird-voice-sweetened by
blackbirds and the frantic gabble-tongues of young
starlings ganging together, then slow-curling over
our heads in their mottled widespread glimmer-net of
wings where fuchsia, ferns, gorse, briars, and
bracken blazon their sober greens and spiky
extensions, and where a host of wildflowers and
weeds are elbowed every which way by a sweet
south-easter cooling our hot faces: then it's the sight
of a white flotilla of swans sailing wide-winged and
stately on the nameless lake of light-painted blue on
which their whiteness glows heraldic: and on we go
so, past a clean pasture of self-enraptured heifers
which move in slow motion and—unlike the rest of
us doubt-troubled souls—seem sure of their own
certainties (the ground they stand on, the fact of
grass) though they too will be fooled in the end by
what's ahead of them: then we're crossing seawards
again and there's the ease of going into a great
silence broken only by the soft aura-slap of the light
breeze against our ears and by the high-pitched
whine of flies, gold-flecked, cruising the ruins of St
Feichín's church, as their fly ancestors haunted its
stony nooks and singing aisles, when brown-cowled
tonsured monks (wrapped against the cold of a

wintry blast or the salt-burn of a good summer) circled chanting . . . and it's here we snap photos of the three of us together before entering once again into the good air-engrossing silence, each of us remembering our own dead . . . and on so, over the green strands of grass (sheep-cropped, breeze-shaken) till we stop to admire the single brilliance of the bright candle-heads of yellow asters, and to force a foot-crushed clump of chamomile to release its scent like a blessing of incense to us where we stand in the ordinary, daily-changing, everlasting island air.

No Words

Living from long minutes of silent meditation
to minutes of browsing brawny mouthfuls of
weeds and grass and wildflowers (mustard,
buttercup, clover, dock), they occupy a uni-
verse of time I can neither know nor enter,
where they (this chalk-white Connemara
mare and her spindle-legged, dark-eyed, clay-
colored daughter) stretch their massive heads
over the stone wall we two are sitting beside
in sunshine, and nuzzle our outstretched oat-
filled palms, and show their mouthfuls of
goofy huge teeth and the long wet curve of
their lapping tongues, and I see the slow
stately swivel of their swan-neck-balanced
heads and the bulky curve of belly and back
and the sudden swish of their tails (yellow
and chestnut) flicking, flouncing, or
tossing—unconscious as any girl's—as they
stroke each other head to head or lip to flank:
icons of such tender affection that the heart
might tremble at it, seeing its deep, complete
unselfconscious satisfaction, as if they are
conducting a conversation on the astral plane:
so in tune with each other that it only needs
the tiniest shiver of skin to say everything
needed: as can only seldom happen in the
sphere where we others must deal mindfully
each minute with *what's to be said? what's
possible? how?* . . . though taken at rare

intervals out of ourselves as we two are now, simply watching these creatures be as they are and absorbing even a fragment of their pure worldliness: ocean-full with all the flickering wonder that words won't touch, and none the worse for it.

Respite

When I saw the small brown bird (chaffinch or
sparrow or dunnock) enter and vanish into the
leafy branch I'd intended to cut from our young
oak, so the tree would be lightened and send
more of its green energy up the bulking trunk, I
had second thoughts, seeing how the birds had
made their own of it, passing part of their secret
lives in its green shade where 'safety' would be
the word we'd have for the feeling they'd feel in
there, and so I put the saw away and lay out on
the deck-chair in an interval of unlikely sun-
shine, a "pet day" between two storm-swept
days of August, and simply lay there listening to
whatever live voices were translating ordinary
air to song . . . and (with my own eyes closed)
feeling something of that same safety the birds
might feel (out of near danger and beyond, for a
little while, hunger) and so feel at home in their
own huge solitude, making the most of it, as I
myself would make the most of it, watching
with half-closed eyes the slow solemn dance
those quick air-awakened responsive oak-leaves
perform, with their maternal branch (still uncut)
determining, conductor-like, every trembling,
pointed moment.

Gannet

That gannet patrolling the tempest-tossed whirl-blasted air off the foreshore has to beat southeast against the southeast gale to achieve elevation, then banks, swoops low on slim stiff wings, to rise once more and scan open water: the snow-white, whiter than sea-foam widespan of its two wings down-gliding to shave dark water and rise again, again on upbeating wings, in the aerodynamic beauty of flesh, feather, flight, to be a single thing of wonder when it stops a second still aloft then stoops and plunges: a thick white missile with black wingtips pointed head and yellow beak all miraculously assembled into one single sharp light-snagging killing machine clean-cleaving the surface and vanishing with hardly a splash—just a small white curdling of water so I can see nothing but dark flat water far out and (in closer) the sea's undulant pale green over sandy shallows . . . till the bird breaks back to this storm-beaten day in which I walk the empty shoreline to watch it begin again patrolling, waiting, holding fast: an assemblage of yellow-eyed patience and oaring wing—keen, eager-eyed, every feather intent for its next entrance.

Rhyming with Beckett

When I stumbled, then tripped with a jolt, over the rhyme between *ontology* and *oncology*, a little window opened like an aperture in a Beckett play for voices, through which we may peer and peer and see nothing, or rather see the Nothing that is blackness itself and no easing it, so you draw a kindly veil and keep talking as if your very own life—endangered species as it is—depended on it, which of course it does, since that external babble you are trying not to overhear is not the sound of *the multitudinous dialects* and *twitter-tongues of all the nations of birds*, no, but the nocturnal *clash* of *ignorant armies* taking care of things—*oncology* and *ontology* among them—along with the small scream-sounds bleeding from the open mouths of the likes of us: we captive audiences who get willynilly caught up in the whole unstaunchable rigmarole and swept away in it, laughing maybe, but (wouldn't you say?) beyond any final slow-dimming spotlight of hope or expectation.

Two Hares

The dead one lies sprawled at the edge of the road by the ragged green verge of grass, buttercups and weeds in an attitude of sleep, its head tucked under forepaws as if to block out this sudden bad that has happened, wringing all the good light out of everything: the day itself, the two gleaming onyx eyes, the brain that was never still till it was done, then nothing to be done about it. Earlier this morning I'd seen the live one, a young one, pause outside our bedroom window and nibble with infinite *delicatesse* the fresh parsley sprouts sprung from a patch of brown earth, then turn its attention to some nodding anonymous green weed-stalks and blades of rass and—when it stopped to look about—I could see the chalk-white triangular blaze staining its forehead, and see, too, how all the rinsed light of the rain-swept day this creature seemed so at home in, was shining out of its two onyx-bright, live, ready-for-anything eyes.

Sieve

Because I've been sieving from carrageen
its health-giving honey-colored juices and
spilling the seaweed sludge into the
kitchen bin, I'm reminded of my mother's
sieve with its round frame of light-
colored wood held circular with a central
hasp of black metal, and I can see her
figure bent intently over it, one hand
holding it steady while the other stirs and
sifts down with a wooden spoon whatever
mash of potatoes, carrots, stewed onions
and a sprinkling of thyme she'd serve as
that day's soup, the sound of that brown
old wooden spoon scraping the wire mesh
seeping into and settling (fertile as any
sedimentary seed-bed) forever in my
head. Table-high, I'm watching her and
feeling . . . what? Her simple solid near-
ness, I suppose: a body of flesh and blood
and hands and concentrated face, which
she turns down now to my own up-
looking child-face, gives a half-smile,
then gets on with what she's doing:
making soup, making a life she went on
making as long as there were mouths to
feed and energies to burn. No talk except
the occasional—when I'd reached too
far—*Mind your hand, love* . . . or—when
it was all done and simmering in the

aluminum saucepan I still keep right here in the cottage—a satisfied sigh of *There now,* or a good-humored *It'll be ready soon; think you can wait?* Then off she'd hurry to check the dining-room table, glancing into the bright oval of the mirror there, where her eyes and her furrowed forehead appear for a passing instant and then vanish.

Keepsake, Inishmore

In one of this island's cherished legends
Heart-troth was a word the saint used,
and you heard it echoing again on the
salted air in the middle of the graveyard
where, buried deep in sand, stands the
island's oldest church. There, in the
long-ago of legend, saint and penitent
had stood together, having bowed low
through the narrow doorway as full
morning sun broke through two pointed
windows to make the gray, rough-rock
building blocks shine bright as the scar-
let poppies and the blue and bright pink
night-scented stock still nodding in the
clean breeze off the sea that was then,
as now, a sheet of beaten brass beyond
the walls of the cemetery, which you
enter now and step between the rows of
weed-wreathed crosses to remember all
those island dead at rest in their own
native-tongued island clay. *Heart-troth,*
so, is what you've kept fresh: like a
small plucked poppy burning its furious
furnace-red in the dark of your own
otherwise empty pocket.

Folk Memory

That doleful one-note cry of a nightbird
might be Mad Sweeney, branch-perched
between our sycamore, oak, and ash: one
note only—plaintive, constant, pitched
high-helpless and at a loss in its sea-deep
unassuageable distress . . . the way you
might any minute expect a face at your
dark fire-flickering window—some bare
deposed soul crying over his kingdom
gone—relentless the cry of him, poor
lost creature abroad among branches:
ash, oak, and sycamore bending to him,
but no annealing repeal nor any
redemption at all offered anywhere this
wind-vexed voice-haunted outcast night.

The Rain Maiden

What is the story I wondered at in the old days?
The one about a woman who manifested out of
mist when the house under its solid dome of rain
had grown (though it was midday) dark as night,
and there's a soft tapping on the skylight first,
then at the tight-closed door, and then when you
open it, there standing in her own silver cape of
rain she is, and she simply comes in to you just
like that—like the surprise of a dear cousin
come back all unbeknownst from overseas—and
wherever her eyes light is all of a sudden bright as
light itself is, and even the risen wind has a
softer whisper so you can hear the storm—
although not yet passed—is abated, and then
you'd feel this rich uncanny silence fill the
house and you'd feel at ease in it and so you'd
make her welcome, though she would say
nothing—nothing but the old blessing: *God save
all here.*

Grace

It was the slow motion of the mare's
swan-neck and massive head as she
turned to the sound of my steps on
the road outside her stonewalled
field that reminded me not only of
the restrained grace of a tai chi
master, but of the way the mind
can—given half a chance of solitude
and that kind of replenishing absence
that takes you once in a while
beyond the borders of the
burdensome flesh and into some
other zone—the mind, as I say, can
achieve at last some given condition
of ease: like this mare who's lost, it
seems, in the depths of
contemplation yet aware of me there,
and can hold both states in some sort
of tranquil oblivious equilibrium and
be at last at peace (or some equine
equivalent) in that neat ring of grass
and buttercups she stands so still in
that I wonder what she knows herself
to truly be then—pure and simple
horseness itself—and I wonder too, as
I start walking away in my own (for
the moment) uncastable and non-
exchangeable complex body, wonder
how far away from such a state I am,

even if it's only a state of beckoning
haze I keep my two live and patient
and (for the moment) wide-awake
eyes on.

Rain Cows

Silent and stolid and sullen-looking under the spilling rain these six cows have made a mucky black mash of the field path again, but what I'm really noting as I trudge in my wellingtons uphill to the top gate is how the rain has beaded on their black, brown, khaki-colored cowhides, the way it will (after a shower) on roses and fuchsia flowers in the garden, jewelling the place when the sun comes out again: and though now there's no sun to turn the cows' rainy veil of sequins into the dozen dew-colors of any sunlit summer morning, yet these droplets are still the bright-est presences to catch my eye this dark, rain-sodden day—brighter even than the glint of the dozen golden flies that have landed to feast on the neat olive-green cowpat splatted pancake-flat in the middle of the path . . . which I avoid stepping in on my way up, then downhill back to the house, under the unflustered gaze of six stolid, steady, earth-anchored, cloven-hoofed creatures, who shift not an inch out of my careful way, but who have seen all this a thousand and more times before, and felt it all, and known and know it simply as the way things, all unquestioned, simply are.

Biblical Wisdom

While the Lord Himself may grant shelter
from the sharp wind to the shorn lamb,
it's hard to see how this desolate creature
half-black half-white standing half-shorn
by a rusted fence, with its tattered fleece
flapping in the wind that's making shards
of rosebushes and forcing fuchsia twigs
to take flight across the glittergreen flurry
of grass, can take much consolation from
such tempering sentiments, no more than
I can myself, caught out as I am in this
stiff tempest of contradictions, the gale
blowing all I know this way and that, and
no way—as this stricken lamb knows
(shivering in the untempered misery of its
own lamb knowledge)—no way but by a
draught of animal patience to withstand it
all, all this buffeting, this way of the
world and its weather . . . and so we
wait—this half-shorn lamb and I—until
there's a little relenting in this indifferent
relentlessness and maybe, just maybe, the
slight off-chance of an even incomplete
rainbow, a shaft of sunlight and promise
fighting its way to glory: the way, after a
solid week of driving rain that shakes
everything to the bone, comes the sudden
intervention of a sunny upright cluster of
tall foxgloves, trim and jaunty-purple,
coming into blossom.

On the Far Side of the Thornbush

Stands a ragged green field arrayed with buttercups, daisies, and a small settlement of recent yellow irises springing out of brown pony-dung, where the white pony slow-swivels his hieratic head in my direction; full-stopped, he surveys me up and down, then slow-turns and is a slow-motion (for the moment) creature until, with an electric twitch, he sudden-gallops to become a beast of fire, until the barbed wire stops him in his madcap pony-tracks, so he offers one quick interrogative whinny at my departing shape: his large, lonesome, sphere-deep black eyes finding my receding shape and—with those flicking ears and fixed inquisitive gaze—following.

Glass

(In the Hardware Shop)

When I caught the chaffinch in my cupped hand
it had just come up against the transparent fact
of glass and was fast-flapping its puzzled in-
dignation athwart the mystery that was bright
and see-through and hard at once, so nothing to
be done but batter wild wings at it—like a man
meeting some sudden impossible-to-resolve stop
in the life he's taken up to this for granted and
who can do nothing about it but take account of
his heart in its startlement as it flutters to the
drumbeat of its deep tachycardiac surprise, and
he thinks how it's like what a trapped wing-
flapping chaffinch with no outlet might feel
while slapping glass, until to its scared surprise
a hand (warm soft strange) takes it in hand and
holds it for a few enormous seconds of silence
broken only by three sharp cheeps of terror and
then slow-opens and the sudden outside air is
bright without obstruction and the creature lifts
off and lets the glitterwind take it and it's gone
so, and my hand goes back to its own business
of buying nails while the shopman who's seen it
all happen remarks: "Birds—ah they never seem
to get it, do they . . . glass?"

Dance

Two small wall-brown butterflies
shape a tiny gyre of wheeling and
twirling above their own twirling
and wheeling black shadows cast
on the grassed-over gravel at the
cottage door: they never touch
but go on and on in bewildering
loops and spirals, closer than one
inch apart: it must be a mating
ritual, I think, for they won't call
any pause or halt: two cloaked
dervishes in their own revol-
utionary dance of, I suppose,
desire, without once touching;
then, as if at some given signal,
one of them all of a sudden
breaks away from their common
unwidening gyre, in which they
have been turning and turning,
and arcs off into the shade of the
gable, leaving its mate solo, to
draw slow circles alone for a
moment or two until it too, still
slow-fluttering, slopes off and
I—with their dance done—am
left sitting here with these words
the only applause I can offer for
their full-bodied, soulful (is that
it?) performance.

Burial

When with the big garden fork I lifted
the ripped-open corpse of the hare I was
surprised by the light weight of it as I
carried it away from the spot, its own
rawly   red-as-fuchsia   lifeblood   still
dripping from the open wound in its
stomach, while the brown fur clotted
round its headless neck and the slick
sheen of its fist-big undamaged liver
stayed gleaming in the sun of June as
the creature composed a once-and-for-
all show of its most secret self to the
world when I tossed it (all slim legs and
perfect feet, its trim back fur-matted,
chalk-white, ash-brown) into the dense
shadow-clump of a furze bush of eye-
startling yellow, where it fell with a
strangely solid heavy-earthed *thump* on
hitting the sodded grass where it will lie
and by degrees get on with its death,
while the chaffinches and bluetits that
perch on our feeder will (it's their
nature) sing out over the spot where the
hare met the black mink's lethal teeth,
and black silence fell on the creature
that alive is all one sprint-dash, nerve,
and knacky swerve, bringing—on each
of its morning visits—our garden to
life: an unbridled wild energy (part fear,
part ecstasy) alight in its two quick-
bright almost perfectly knowing eyes.

Landscape with Ghost

See that man there—that one crooking both arms as
he swings his scythe through the long grass that's a
mass of pink flowers I've no name for, that one
stripped to the waist for action with half the field in
flat pink swathes behind him, his field yes half-
shorn, the field in front of that house where sixteen
years ago the son of the house (a young man in his
twenties) died, and where last night his mother had
a dream in which there was a knock at the door and
when she answered it he walked in and grinned and
said *Hi Mam, I'm back* . . . and she woke and knew
it was a dream: and still the scythe-man goes on
laying flat the field, his instrument a clean sweeper
of that living pink space till he stops for breath and
stands honing the blade, then bends again to his
cutting and cutting down, while the wind goes on
taking the low *swishhh* and *swishhh* of the falling
grass and those falling anonymous pink flowers as
if they weighed nothing—nothing—away with it.

Nature Vivant: Just Looking

(Bonnard: *Paysage du Midi*)

North to Normandie or down south to some
flowering corner of the Midi hardly matters when
you stand in front of this Bonnard that—as if a
controlled explosion of color—can blow your doors
of perception wide open, seeing (as you give
yourself over to it) how the labor of his two eyes, not
to mention the palpitating rest of him (head to heart
and heart on a downslope towards the seat of
whatever it is that propels one into simple wanting,
the ache of appetite), makes you scramble now for
ways to take it in, saying to yourself *how can I taste
and swallow this in all its spectral illuminations, all
exactly calibrated, so what is natural gives way to
what his excited but unblinking eye and biddable
hand makes up*: a shining fiction filled to brimming
with its own kind of truth, the throb of it through the
hot kiln of the seen, the whole scene-scape
encompassing, no, *dramatizing,* what was simply
standing still before him when he'd walked out that
first—yes—first morning, sketchbook in hand and
took dictation from the facts—from all the greens
(lime, sage, pine) and mesmerizing blues (a topmost
sky of lilac dashes, snatches of palest violet, a blur of
aquamarine close-lurking between navy-blue and
lime-green branches), and even from that cornered
inch of whitewashed wall roof-slated black, with its
square of pale gray-blue-curtained window keeping
its own discreet human vigil on the radical
abundance and raw confusion in this riot of

photosynthesis (as uncentered as for the moment God is), and still you go on looking and looking into some untidy but meaning-laden shapes of shadow limned into the enigma of *negative space* and a single square of *pointilliste* lilac and rose splotches along with eye-caressing zones of yellow—from mimosa to witch hazel, from amber to ochre to honeyed gold—while a few warm accent-spots of burnt orange edge into a gathering of dark green-browns of bark and the lighter brown of what we used to call French mustard . . . and look there, where (sprouting out of a dark daub that speaks out loud *the sensuality of shade*, like refugees sprung from another kind of garden) spring the tips of two tiny isolated flowerheads asserting their poppy-red intensity, minute but eye-catching, for they are (along with two even tinier droplets near them) the single tinctures of red in the whole exuberant deranged arrangement (with its glinting galactical star-particles of random, untempered, *onlie begetter* light itself), contained but no way restrained by the plain canvas rectangle he must have left pinned to his studio wall in *Le Cannet* or wherever for a tempering, a burgeoning age while he sentry-walked to and fro in front of it—now near, now far, with brush in hand; a tip here, another dash there, elsewhere a sudden deliberate heavy-handed laying-on of flesh-thick olive-green among the upper reaches of what remains a vari-hued nameless tree, and so reviving it through all the rapt, slow or rapid, happy procedures of what he lived for: his rooted, modest, insistently assertive, endlessly astonishing, once and for all all-comforting all-unsettling word-defeating resurrection game.

A Visitation

In a warm June breeze our sycamore casts
flickering shadows across the gravel path
so they catch my sidelong eye behind this
big window and I imagine a figure dressed
in daisy-white and sunlight and the rose-red
of a single small geranium shivering in the
window-box; it is a shadow-flicker figure,
as intimate and as strange as a moment's
visitation, a ghostly good presence flit-
ting into my ken and gone before I have a
chance to figure it out. But fair enough, I
think, to stand even for an instant in this in-
between place—liminal and brimming with
possibility, as if some hapless ghost shook
off the grave that stayed it from ordinary
light and time and space, and offered itself
up in our here and now, making the day
stop beating quotidian time and hold its
breath, so everything in it is turned inside
out, though quick as winking the moment is
in the past and all is as before, as I step
from the living-room and look into the
commonplace reassurance of the untransub-
stantiated kitchen and resume my own one
daily life again, as if nothing had happened.

Local

M'illumino d'immenso is what the dream-scribe had inscribed
on the steel door leading out of my last oneiric maze before
waking and walking out into a day neither immense nor in any
way illuminated, but grey as the slick seal's round-snouted
hound-head addressing me with big black glaucous grief-
struck eyes yesterday on Glassillaun, where I'm caught in ear-
thrall to the hollow melodic out-of-sight but unmistakable
snipe's snare-drum solo as it plummets from on high, all
gimlet-eyed self-belief braving reckless descent at such speed
it is a miracle of focus or some concentrated something we've
no word for: simply being a real presence we take—like any
other aureoled belief—on trust for its single bewildering
moment . . . until I'm transported back to this grounded world
of bog-brown, rough-cut, fence posts dangling like broken
gibbets over air where the coastline has been in great grass-
green masses eroded from under them—their tangles of
barbed wire hanging useless, noose-like, and rusted to the
russet of a dead foxpelt. Taking them in too, I stop to listen to
a solitary invisible skylark going crazy again in the clear air—
so not to let go its hold on morning or its own throat-music—
simply voicing what is here now: a few sky-blue slashes
tempering with promise the far-flung cloud-massed gray, to
help me feel (if only for the moment) a trace of something
somewhere somehow immense and (even in this its
diminished local incarnation) illuminated.

Parents

When I heard the pair of oystercatchers shrieking in the high wind blowing the green slopes of Glassillaun every which way as they complained and complained, abusing me as invader of their land-space, hovering on flutterwings, then shearing off over the rock-spurs, then back again still screeching their barrage of parental rage (part protective, part simple vehemence of feeling), the wind all the time shaking the grass, the sharp light picking out purple clumps of wild thyme and a few pale pink bee orchids at my feet—then I thought how absolute instinct was, propelling the rage of these small creatures of air and rock and water to a fury that sets their hearts on fire, igniting such shrill unarguable urgency in voices that never paused nor diminished in intensity till I turned and returned the way I'd come into their own kingdom and so left them in peace and total possession, quieted by my visible absence from their small circumscribed native world in which they'd been living hour by hour in that parent-protected peace I had so rudely shattered until driven off by their raucous outbursting opposition, till they knew the coast was clear and the nest was safe, and would remain so as long as they could breathe and fly and screech their manic heads off, until their hapless hidden fledglings learned their own fierce-hearted way in the always endangered, endangering world.

Old Habit

Quarter moons, she'd call them, cradling my small hand in her big freckled hand and pushing down with a single sharp fingernail the cuticle of my thumb, then index, middle, ring, and little finger—and there it would be every time: a clean white quarter moon between cuticle and nail, and always a surprise, as was the feel of her hand holding mine like that, hardly any thought to it, just the handhold that was as natural as her face bending over my half-awake face in the early morning light and saying as soft as she could, so not to wake my sleeping brothers: *Time to get up, love, you're serving Mass at eight* . . . and I'd rise and dress in silence while she in her flowered nightie padded back to bed to lie still beside my still sleeping father . . . *Quarter moons*, indeed, and I'd note how she'd do it at odd times for herself: holding her own hand and talking— about nothing important most likely—and gently touching her thumbnail to each of her own fingernails in turn, the act as natural as breathing, as the rise and fall of her voice, as the light coming through the living-room window to wrap itself around the two of us, before I'd take a breath and dash off and out and leave her there alone and looking at her hands: at the live-flashing ruby ring and the diamond engagement ring and the tight gold wedding ring glinting on them.

Self Portrait with Yellow Raincoat

At first it's gold of gorse and gray fieldstones
giving their all to this rocky landscape, then I'm
in the vast elemental lonesomeness of the
Roundstone Bog, where glitter-mirrors of lake
after lake create the deep gleams of a world
given over to mirage, and where the pale snake
of a sunlit stream between one bright body of
water and another makes a pause, until
suddenly I'm out of all that openness, and into
the peaceful green enclosures of trees, cropped
fields, stone walls with their green hands of
ferns waving at me in passing, and some last
orange embers not of daylight but montbretia
glinting at the verge of roads and hedges, and
then it's the sheer comfort of four Connemara
ponies (two white mares and a brown and a
black foal) suddenly sighted racing across the
slope of their hedge-bound pasture—manes
and tails flying in the crosswind like the blown-
back foam of whitecaps rising and racing to
their own consummation on the tideline of the
White Strand, where yesterday (with the sky all
coppery light, and the wet sand streaked with
opal and pearl where the tide had drawn back)
I could glimpse suddenly my daughter in her
visionary lemon raincoat walking towards me
through pools of pale mauve, over which I
found myself hurrying to meet her.

Skin Deep

Last night our most common simple surface
made me shiver with dismay at the simple
mystery of skin—the sting of it—how it
holds its ache. Wasp, tick, nettle, no matter:
the throb endures like a trace of thunder,
the distant deep grumble of its drawing off.
The way, too, skin will continue to foster
its minor blaze, its gremlin embering—the
way embers (under ash the morning after)
go radiant, you know how it is, with the
merest breath. So be wary, *non toccare,* or
all will then again be blaze, a quickened
conflagration, and divil a bit any balm or
unguent would do the trick. *O skin,* your
dream-brain hums through heated silence
of the night, *be now my ally, now, and give
over your long haul of ache and sting, your
deep residue of unfriendly edginess—for I
would be whole again, airy as ever, fancy-
free of all such stiletto-tip invasions—be
simple pause and panacea, and free me into
wholeness once more, and by morning be
unthrobbing: whole, hale and emancipated:
once more made ordinary, starting over.*

With Ant and Celan

This tiniest mite of an ant, no bigger
than a full stop, is making its careful
way across a poem by Celan and
stopping to inspect with its ant feelers
(can it smell or see? is all in the idiom
of touch?) each curve of each letter,
knowing nothing of the mill of
thinking that ground into it, into each
resonant syllable of each word. The
ant stops on *Sprache* and sniffs at its
ins and outs, its blank whites and
curlicues of black, then moves on to
the next word, *Sprache*, and busies
itself with its own ant-brand of
understanding; but finding nothing of
what it seeks it moves to the blank
margin of nothing more, stumbles
over the edge of the page and I have
to imagine it is saying (if that's the
word) to itself something that
translated means *No food. Nothing
here* . . . And so now, gone back into
its own weird world of stones and
weeds and grass and sun-shadows, it
is lost to me as I go back into the dark
wood of Celan's poem—a world of
words I feel my diligent way through,
sniffing at its tangle of branches, its
brief sun-flower flashes: *Language,*

language, it will sing in translation: *Partner-Star* . . . *Earth-Neighbor. Poorer. Open* . . . Then: *Homelike. Homely. Homelandlike. Heimatlich.* And so I take its final word to heart, the way that most minuscule creature might take back to its own earth- burrow a seed, a scrap of anything either edible or useful, anything it could translate to nourishment, and live a little with it.

With Curlews and Starlight

Remembering the three curlews I saw this morning over windy Gurteen, and hearing the high notes of their mournful comeback, I stumble again into the curious exactitudes marking time and tide, seeing how these local migrants make (regular as calendar clockwork and against the awful odds of their extinction) their annual return to this strand, these fields: whole long-legged, brown-feathered, curve-beaked flocks of them buoyant and purposeful in their clear-sounding sweep across a clouded sky. Now, though, it's silent night—only a dog barking—and the cleared sky has filled the dark with stars for the first time in weeks, so I stand outside, compelled as any other creature by the slow cloud-lift to obey a nameless instinct and look up open-mouthed, while the now-silenced sleeping curlews—indifferent or not they may be to starlight—are bedded elsewhere, in bushes or field hollows or among sea-rock crevices: one side of their collective brain awake, one vigilant eye open, so no prowler, no hoverer, no marauding sky-swooper (obeying time and its own punctual, present, biting hunger) can—endangered as they are already—snatch them.

Tangle

Little lethal goldbeaks and all varieties of
yellow-winged green flashings are at their
hungry work now, now the garden's been
flooded by last night's noisy torrents of
rain cascading in streams along the
gutters we've constructed, where the wet
mud's a flourishing seedbed for risen
earthworms and other wrigglers the birds
love to batten on . . . Such a tangle this
state of things: good for the birds feasting
on live morsels the rain has brought them;
bad for the garden drowning under the
unsparing rain; and very bad for the
worms stopped in their own mid-ecstasy
relishing the fresh mud, the life-giving
swill of it. From my morning's exalted
perch by this tall rain-glazed window I
oversee the lot of it.

At the Heart of Things

When out of the smothering wet muck
of dead leaves choking the gutter after
a hard winter, a honeybee big as my
thumb, its body furred black and
yellow, rose in fright and whirring
indignation, buzzing to beat the band,
and circling my head for a second or
two then drifting off to find in this
short burst of sudden sunshine another
place to get on with the life it's been
given . . . it left me alone and ladder-
perched to get on with mine—each of
us bent as necessary to our tasks: me
making a clean passage for rainwater
to run clear into the downpipe and on
into the earth, the bee prospecting for
nectar among the bright yellow and
white "poached-egg" flowers: each of
us, so, intent in our own small ways to
help the world advance, run on—and
to achieve and flourish the way nature
—*God help us!*—intended.

Spirit Glimmer

Arse in the air, rest of him sunk head-first
among the innards of an injured car (a
Peugeot) my honest garage-man is getting
on with his life, a life buried for days in the
entrails of trucks, cars, engines, with a sick
child ever on his mind, so he gets on with it,
a genial spirit making do, the way the tree
I'm passing (a bent wind-flayed sycamore)
makes do whatever the weather (day by day,
moon-full by moonless night) delivers, and
has grown, so, into the graceful shape of a
lithe dancer, as if there's some refining truth
in endurance: the way that sudden goldfinch
lights out of the tangle of a brown thornbush
I'm passing, and perches a moment on the
rusting barbed wire fence before lifting off
to become a brief flame-colored dazzle,
taking broad morning light to itself before
vanishing as it has to into its uncountable
coming moments, while I—in the flash and
grasp of my own given moment—drive on
along the winding Corrywongaun road
toward Tully Cross, then Tully, then home.

Fire Time: An Act of Hope

(For Rachel)

It is the way the fire of turf blazes up, then turns
to a mute incandescent rose inside a dark brown
shell that has set me thinking about time and
how tricky an element it is which we walk and
swim and even fly about in, how it lives on what
will be the death of it, a going toward nothing
that I might say I'd want my own end to be: first
blaze, then peaceful heat—so whatever fuel I'd
fed the life I'd led might be a source of light
beyond me and be there when the dark matter
had been flamed away and all that stayed was
the warm rose-tinted comfort of a solid-banked
radiance, a fire that had lived to the full its full
fire-life and still in its going, like the best of
what we say to each other, might—let's say
might—endure beyond its final conflagration,
holding itself to itself and going on to make the
kind of sense fire makes of its best benevolent
self (living as it does off that which is the source
of its own undoing) so we could look in our own
wide-open eyes then and not flinch: just hoping
to take to heart the whole truth of it.

How Things Add Up

The hazeblue fretworked silhouette of Achill
was the second thing I saw this fine morning
as it floated on a sea still as a steel mirror
with a small far-out fishing boat pinned to it
and standing on water as if painted there;
and the third thing I saw was a jetblack and
sand-colored heap asprawl on the strand,
that had been before beaching and dying a
live seal whose coat and skin the ravening
gulls had pocked and bitten into perfect
circles with the awl-sharp tips of their lethal
beaks: headless and with ripped flippers,
like a bulging black bag of wet cement was
this flesh creature that would not stir again
till the coming tide could scoop it into its
arms of foam and salt and draw it back to a
burial too deep for live sky-beaks to
dismantle and batten on. But the first thing I
saw this morning was a pair of jackdaws
perched gaily on a phone-wire and preening
each other with an odd low chuckling, as if
being tickled; they held that one single sun-
struck moment alive and lit up in the
polished gloss of their ebony feathers, and I
took their chuckles for company as I walked
beneath their lilting life and its pure
ongoingness: all that life-giving goodness
happening—once and for all there and then
above me.

Snatched

The little secrets are still all there, they still cast shadows
—Celan

In and out among the stones of the wall
a wren, little troglodyte, moves and is
gone, is back, is gone. Over the field a
quick-jinking twirl of brown finches
catches a breeze, soars, loops, drops,
snatches at the wind again and rises
twittering: it is a diminutive chorus, a
visitation of small music under a sky
swollen with coming rain to douse the
whole island with its solid down-
pouring force, forcing everywhere into
orange alerts, orange as the color of the
dying montbretia and the last of the last
embers in the grate I'm cleaning out to
the music of finches and the quick
corner-of-the-eye sight of that tiny
rock-dweller, the wren, as it skitters
stone to stone and holds, as the finches
hold (but neither montbretia nor the
flickering embers hold) the moment
passing through the lot of us shiverers
in the grip of time, and it's into that
thought I settle, so, brushing the last ash
from the grate, then rise and wash my
hands of it, and get on with the day I'm
passing through that's passing right
through me, and know to raise no fist

against the finality of whatever is out there or in here: all its fire-lit, gone-in-a-wren-blink one life, quick-snatched as it's passing and in vain snatched at.

Two Walking

In this gift of a good day at last, sunshine is a heaven for houseflies and for this small scarlet and black moth crossing our uphill path and fluttering the way a lunatic tongue might in stuttering its own home truths—and we see how all is alight as a pulse running wild with its own delighted sense it's a *now*, a *here* is sun-juice and breeze-soul rolled together and at ease in this blessed riot of glare, the way the shorn lambs are, perched on their grass-green patches high above the stoneblue ridges of Ballynakill, the bay in its ring of hills that remain, in their simple, solid presence an undulant, deep-dark horizon to our gaze with their anonymous ur-burly *thereness*—their weight and great bulk a kind of terminus, uttering their own home truths—*We are forever here, say what you can as you pass: we watch over all you are, and over that wind-bent roof of ash-leaves you pause under in this shimmering day that is your own paired moment too, you pair breathing easy in such benign sensuality of shade* . . . which is when the oracle goes quiet and we proceed, taking this good day in as nourishment—our human viaticum for the ongoing uphill journey—and going on with it.

Return to Inishmore

Luminous morning for a bit, then
the back-cloth of mist takes over
and all luminosity leaves it but for
the bright yellow of mustard and
the bridal white of big daisies
blowing in the island breeze; night
and it's the damp silence of
fieldstone walls making up the
way things are here and now, with
a necklace of lights along the pier
and the sharp star-twinkle of lit
houses constellating the coast of
Connemara; nothing to be done
so, here among the graves with
their tall-standing stone markers:
dead-silent cross-topped sentinels
I passed this morning on my way
along maze-paths beside fields of
long flat granite slabs, the bleed of
cranesbill sudden-starting out of
crevices—the place steady as ever
in its own becoming—urgent and
withholding and ordinary and
unlikely as ever.

Room with Misia

In Vuillard's interior, where the walls are chalkwhite
flecked with yellow, stands a worktable of deal on
which stands a leather-brown container for note-
paper, envelopes, pens, all leaning against an upright
gray square-cut wooden post with angled supports
slotted into a roof-beam of charcoal gray, beside
which a chair—with backrest, cross-slats, and a sea-
blue cushioned seat—barely touches a wicker waste-
basket tucked in against one squared leg of the table,
to the left of which and attached to the wall juts a
ledge or shelf on which (like a small still life) stand a
black ceramic jug, a squat coffee pot, and a curved
pipe, all wearing an air of *we belong*, while (attached
to the wall) there's a painting (maybe Vermeer, a
copy) and a paler unknown one, while the wooden
post has postcards or small sketches pinned to it, and
on the lacquered wooden floor you'll see a segment
of a Turkish rug, its margin of deepest maroon
enclosing a narrow fragment of creamy woven
yellow—and there beside the half-open door (cloud-
grey, with daubs of yellow) there in shadow stands a
woman in a long blue flowered dress who is holding
an open newspaper; her pale auburn-blonde hair is
barely visible in shadow, yet still she is a bright-lit
presence in that containing dusklight: a meditative
observer, she seems to be taking (maybe with the
party over) the room into herself—remembering the
talk, the faces on fire with it and with the wine;
remembering the way the light held each talker and
caressed each brimming wineglass, like a lover's
warm-holding hand.

Broken Wall

panta rhei . . .
—Heraclitus

These fieldstones and big rocks fallen from the rough garden wall in front of our cottage must have come down in last night's heavy rain and lie there like stilled bodies this morning. Trying, without much hope, to set all back in its place, I was thinking as I picked and placed large stones and small—all crooked angles and solid mass—of the man who, with his neighbors, built it first, and I was marveling at how it has stood for a hundred years or so and only now, while I slept, has it fallen—to say in its own stony way how *everything flows*, nothing stays solid forever. The biggest rock, a huge head-shaped mass of granite, resembles a man-creature turned to stone (petrified brow, nose, mustache, cheek, and mouth) and squats there staring in one window at us with a grim half-smile that says: *There's no putting this Humpty Dumpty together again,* and I can think only of the hands that dug in under it and released it from boggy black earth and manhandled it to hoist it into place, an anchor-stone, and saying (in Irish or in English) as they did: *That's it so, and not a budge at all out of it now, is there?* Like any stone idol, the head says nothing, only stares in through the window I'm staring out of at it, and at that makeshift mend I've made in hope, while the fuchsia flowers—like supplicants offering obeisance at one god's altar or another—go on gleaming over it.

Anniversary Mother

And how do *the mute phenomena of the world*
take the big dark to themselves and in stride?
Dew-spangled grassblades, leaves of the great
oak, the ash, the sycamore; hushed patience of
mushrooms edging into light overnight; or the
wild golden eye of the tufted duck . . . not to
mention dustbins and holly berries, or the roses
(blowing or blown or in the bud) we would
take stock of on our walks . . . or the empty
park bench standing silent in the same city park
where we'd sit in silence together, watching the
world go by: the bench a memorial in my mind
now to her patient unexpecting self, now she's
gone (*to heaven*, she'd like me to say)
underground these past twenty-five years of
bewildering *this, that,* and *t'other,* that she (one
way or another) would always say "yes" to,
getting on with her living them, deep in the
ordinary happenstance of accident or design
(all the same to her in the end), just getting on
with it, and again I can hear her laugh with her
heart at something I'd said and saying *Go on,
get along with you!* . . . and I would.

Late Autumn with
Swallows and Sandmartins

This wind-scattered band of swallows swoop-gliding through smooth chutes of air despite the big wind's bluster-gustings that rattle metallic at the green shed on the edge of our neighbor's cow-field, go arrowing from pillar to post in the vicinity of rooftops on open then closed swallow-wings, before slicing the hemisphere of dark that an elbowing corner of that squat rust-red barn offers, into which they vanish. Or a whole chattering family of them congregating on phonewires and fencewires to swap-gossip their own urgent news of the day. Or these three or four sandmartins still here when I walk the White Strand and see them skim over sand and the grey uneven slope of stones, then curling banking swooping at the high wall of the sand-cliff in which their small eye-socket-shaped dwelling-places have been patiently excavated, and into which (like a conjurer's sleight of hand) they vanish. Now all these birds of the air in their excited twittering are a sign of how September has caught up with them and they're taking its signals in, teaching their fledged young how to read the signs: to know from the touch of the sun and its late-afternoon inclination how, in no time now, it will be time to go . . . so that one calm afternoon a bit like this one—

with sunshine bringing out the glitter of mica in the sand—I'll sit here solo, the place vacant but for myself and a few flies inspecting the warm skin of my bare hands, and no brown wings or twitter-voices to keep me company, nor any purple or white wing-flashes to liven the shadows of the barn and the shed next door, its own stony, dark-gaping vacancies a reminder only, as autumn at last puffs up to its last gasps this fulfilled finale blaze of earth, air, and water colors all about me.

White Strand Performance

Behold now the airy dynamic miracle of the man dragged at high speed over choppy water by the great red arc of his parasail kite, its wires snapping in the brisk nor'wester, the breaking waves snatching at the board he's latched to: taut as bowstrings his arms, his legs braced as guy ropes to a tent the wind might lift and whip across the Killary—but he hangs on, no . . . he *exults* in his controlling wind and wild water like this, so that at intervals and hissing speed he'll leap above gaping water, spin a full circle in air, then land again—a landlubber no longer but at home in the elements of air and water, blazing his own way between them, tense and expectant as he is, missing nothing (no twitch of wind, no sudden toss of wave) but riding all opposing forces, so they gather him into this poise that is an exactly achieved dynamic equilibrium, a state almost out of this world but not, so elementally compounded as it is: all human flesh and bone, all muscle, head and heart gathered into this one space-time absolute, until the wind dies and the kite flags, sags, dips to water, and the man lets it happen, feels the not unkindly touch of water, sinks into it, and floats there, almost at rest, scanning the almost empty shore.

Hare at Dusk

Knacky swift and dashing as ever, the hare
that manifests all of a sudden in the windy
dusk that is taking over the rock-rugged
cowfield I walk by is disappeared as soon
as seen, gone under the metal gate and
through my neighbor's garden, and gone,
gone again as on a raw electric current of
aliveness: but gone—as the dusk that is
fast becoming hare-colored will soon be
gone too, lost to the deeper dark of the
night while the storm's big breath goes
howling over lamb-cry and lost-calf cry.
But the hare is safe away by now from it
all, hunkered down in some scented hedgy
dip or hollow, or in the lea of any
windstruck rock, where it can listen to its
heart's quick insistent little drumming as it
gathers itself into the blood-warm cell of
itself: its form and refuge till the big dark
blows over.

ACKNOWLEDGMENTS

Acknowledgments are due to the editors of the following publications where some of these poems, or versions of them, were published first: *Agni, Beloit Poetry Journal, Birmingham Poetry Review, Cyphers, diode, The Gettysburg Review, The Hampden-Sydney Poetry Review, The Hudson Review, The Irish Times, Poetry, Smartish Pace, The St. Ann's Review, The Stinging Fly, Terrain,* and *The Yale Review.*

Many thanks to Peter Fallon and Gallery Press for their publication of the Irish version of Plainchant. Their unfailing loyalty to my work over the years has always given me great encouragement and satisfaction.

And thanks to the editors at Red Hen Press for their care with the design and presentation of this collection.

The Celan poem quoted on p. 51 is "What Occurred?" ("*Was geschah?*") in *Poems of Paul Celan*, translated by Michael Hamburger, Persea Books, NY, 2002.

The words *m'illumino d'immenso* on p. 46 are from the poem "Mattina" by Giuseppe Ungaretti.

On p. 26, *multitudinous dialects* and *twitter-tongues of all the nations of birds* are phrases from Derek Walcott's poem, "The Season of Phantasmal Peace," and *clash* of *ignorant armies* is from Matthew Arnold's "Dover Beach."

BIOGRAPHICAL NOTE

Born in Dublin in 1941, Irish poet Eamon Grennan taught at Vassar College in Poughkeepsie, NY, for over thirty years. His many volumes of verse have been published in Ireland and the United States since the 1980s. *Still Life with Waterfall* won the Lenore Marshall Poetry Prize in 2003, and his translation of the poems of Leopardi won the PEN Translation award in 1998. *There Now*, his latest book, won the Irish Pigott Prize for poetry in 2016. Grennan's poems have appeared over the years in many American and Irish journals, including *The New Yorker, Poetry Ireland, The Irish Times, Poetry London, TLS, The Threepenny Review, Yale Review, Terrain,* and many others. He has also published a collection of critical essays, *Facing the Music: Irish Poetry in the 20th Century,* and (with his partner, Rachel Kitzinger) translations of Sophocles's *Oedipus at Colonus* and *The Women of Trachis.* For the past ten years he has also been writing and directing short plays on Irish subjects for the Curlew Theatre Company based in the west of Ireland. He lives in Poughkeepsie and Connemara.